The Bear

Story by
ANGELA SHEEHAN

Pictures by
MICHAEL ATKINSON

Exeter Books

NEW YORK

The hillside glowed red as the sun sank behind the tall pines. The bear lumbered through the trees, picking handfuls of juniper berries as she went. Winter was on the way and there was not so much food in the forest now. All the animals had been gathering stores of winter food or eating extra to see them through the cold weather.

At the edge of the trees, the bear stopped. Below her, she could just make out the shapes of a herd of moose on the move. They were too far away for the bear to attack. So she just watched them. Suddenly she heard the sound of a twig snapping behind her. She turned. A branch swayed as a woodpecker, frightened by the noise, hurriedly left its perch. Nothing else stirred.

The bear looked hard, and at last saw what had made the noise – a young moose. It had stayed behind to eat the thick moss on the tree trunks. Now it stood, quivering with fear, watching the bear loping towards it. The young creature screamed to its mother as the bear struck. Then it slumped, dead, to the ground.

The bear was about to drag the body away when another branch swayed and a shaggy, black animal leaped to the ground. It was a wolverine. The creature bared its teeth and growled at the bear. The bear backed away at first and then tried to reach the deer. But even though the wolverine was smaller than her, it drove her back. It was late in the day and the bear was too tired to fight. So she left her kill to the savage wolverine.

As the weather grew harsher, food grew
scarcer. The sun shone for only a few hours each
day. The bear found a deep hollow in the rocks and
made a bed of leaves and moss. Snowstorms turned
the world outside to white, as the bear settled
down for a long sleep.

On some days during the winter the sun
came out for long enough to warm the entrance to
the cave. Then the bear stirred in her sleep or even
woke and came out to see if the winter was over.
One day she was wakened by a squirrel being
chased by a pine marten over the rocks of her den.

Another day, a fox strayed into the den looking for food. The bear chased it away and took a look outside. The snow was still deep and she could find no food. So she spent a little time sliding down the slope outside her cave and then went back inside. The wind was far too cold for her to stay out for long.

The cubs soon learned what fun it was to play among the flowers, chasing birds, bees and butterflies – and each other. The mother bear watched them all the time. All day long she had to rescue them fron one danger or another, scooping them up in her jaws or shooing them up a tree. They only ran back to her when they wanted some more milk or when they were tired of playing.

Soon they began to learn how to hunt. They already knew from their games how to creep up on each other or pounce from behind a tree. Now their mother showed them how to kill for food. They waited by the entrance to a voles' burrow. But the voles could smell them, so they did not come out. When they moved farther away, the voles did come out, but the cubs were not quick enough to catch them. They watched their mother again and saw how long she waited before pouncing. In the end they both managed to kill a vole.

It was a long time before the cubs managed to kill anything bigger. They were far too scared of the big creatures their mother killed. And every time a small creature ran across their paths, a hawk or an owl would swoop down to catch it before they had a chance. It was far easier to catch caterpillars or raid ants' nests.

One day, they had the most delicious food they had ever tasted. Their mother had been watching the bees that came to feed on the flowers. As soon as she found where they lived, she set off with her cubs at her heels. The three of them marched down to the river bank. There, from a hole near the bottom of an old tree, they heard a buzzing sound, and saw a steady stream of bees flying in and out. Inside the tree was the bees' nest.

The little cubs watched their mother. The bees were buzzing around her head but she took no notice. She poked her paw into the tree and pulled out a sweet, sticky mess of wax cells oozing honey. The bear offered her paw to the little cubs who were trying to bat away the angry bees. One lick of the honey and the cubs forgot the buzzing and the beating wings. They swallowed the sweet liquid and hungrily chewed the bee grubs inside the wax cells.

The bear reached into the tree for another sticky pawful for herself. The angry bees swarmed about the bears. But even the cubs had thick enough fur not to feel their stings. They gorged the grubs and honey and licked their sticky lips.

When the cubs were a little older, the bear let them play in the shallow river water. The weather was hot and the water cooled their fur. They loved splashing among the rocks and tumbling from the bank. Even more, they loved to eat the fishes that their mother caught. The cubs tried hard to copy the way the bear flipped them from the water. But every time they tried, the slippery fishes slithered through their paws.

It was not until the salmon came upstream that the cubs managed to catch their first fish. The salmon had come all the way from the sea, swimming against the flow of the river. They were tired by the time they reached the rocky stream where the bears waited for them. Even the cubs could catch them.

The cubs loved going to the river. There were lots of other bear families to play with: young cubs like themselves, some older ones, and even some big male bears, like the one their mother had mated with the year before.

Late in the summer, the bear began to eat extra food and the cubs did the same. Each day she led them to new clumps of berry-laden bushes. She knew exactly where to find the freshest fruit. The other animals were also collecting food. They grew fatter every day.

Soon almost all the nuts and berries had been eaten. The trees on which they grew turned yellow, red and brown. Only the pines and spruces stayed green. By now, most of the insects had disappeared and the birds had long stopped singing. Many of them had flown south to warmer

lands. In the trees the crossbills pecked at cones and the squirrels built their winter dreys. The badgers gathered extra leaves to line their sets.

The bear took her cubs to the cave she had found the winter before. They helped her collect new moss and leaves to make a bed. Then the three of them snuggled up together and went to sleep. At first, they slept for only a few days at a time; then they slept for a few weeks; then for a month, or more. Sometimes all three of them woke and went out into the snow.

By springtime the cubs had grown quite big, but they still liked to drink their mother's milk. She fed them until early in the summer. Then they began to wander farther and farther by themselves. Sometimes they did not even come back at night. The bear knew that they were big enough and strong enough to look after themselves now.

One day when the young bears were away looking for bees' nests, she found a new mate. Like the first male, he did not stay with her long after they had mated. She spent most of her time on her own, wandering over the hillside. The young bears continued to come and go. But by the end of the summer they had found new homes of their own on another part of the hillside. The bear had fed them and kept them safe for almost two years. Now they could fend for themselves. Next spring she would probably have a new family to bring up.

Bear Facts

Eyes
A bear's sight is unusually poor

Mouth
Teeth are good for both tearing flesh and grinding plant food. Bears will eat almost anything.

Feet
Bears are flat-footed, resting their heels on the ground like people

Ears
Hearing is not especially good

Nose
Sense of smell is well developed

Fur
Brown bears range in color from tan to black

Claws
Long and strong; bears cannot withdraw their claws into their paws as cats can

Few kinds of animals vary as much in color and size as the members of the bear family. Some are black, some brown, some white, some tan colored. Some are large, some small. The brown Kodiak bear of Kodiak Island is more than ten feet long and weighs up to 1500 pounds. The white Polar bear is almost as big. The smallest bears are the Malayan bear and the Spectacled bear of South America.

The brown bear in the story roams the wilder parts of North America, northern Europe and Asia. The male weighs up to 550 pounds and can kill an animal bigger than itself with one blow of its clawed paw. The female is slightly smaller.

Honey Lover
Although it is so powerful and belongs to the carnivore (flesh-eating) group of animals, the brown bear is not always a ferocious hunter. It likes to eat a lot of fruit and other sweet things, especially honey. It uses its massive fighting strength, however, when disturbed by people or other animals.

Dancing Bears
Unlike most other animals, bears walk on the soles of their feet not on their toes. They also move both legs on one side of the body at the same time. This makes them appear to shuffle or lope along, even though they can go fast when they want to.

Bears can also move quite easily standing upright on their hind legs. This enables them to use their front legs as arms, though nobody has actually seen one giving a "bear hug". It is also one reason why bears are used as circus animals; their intelligence makes them easy to train, and, even in the wild, they enjoy playing bear games.

In the Middle Ages in Europe, bears were led through the villages, muzzled and chained, and forced to perform for the amazed onlookers. The cruel practice of baiting bears – teasing them – to make them "dance" has long been banned.

Summer and Winter

In the wild, bears lead solitary lives, except when a mother is bringing up her cubs, which she does with no help from the father. Each bear roams over an area of about 13 square miles, sleeping rough at night during the warmer months.

In winter they find a den and go into a long, fitful sleep. But they do not really hibernate as some animals do; they wake from time to time. The cubs are usually born in winter and are very very small – about 18 ounces and only 8 inches long.

Spectacled bear

Malayan bear
(sun or honey bear)

Himalayan black bear
(moon bear)

Sloth bear

Polar bear

American black bear

Some of the different kinds of bears

More books for you to read from
EXETER BOOKS

WILDLIFE LIBRARY

If you have enjoyed this book, you will
be pleased to know that it is part of a
series:

    The Bear
    The Elephant
    The Deer
    The Wolf

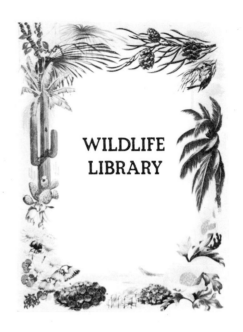

MY FIRST BOOK OF NATURE

In addition, there are six titles in
My First Book of Nature, a companion
series about the smaller creatures of
the countryside:

    The Duck
    The Butterfly
    The Squirrel
    The Fox
    The Frog
    The Mouse

All the books are in full color.